I0749193

Poetry in the Age of Impurity

Poetry
in the
Age of Impurity

Thomas Sanfilip

Bigio Morato

Several essays herein have appeared previously in the following publications: "Poetry *in Extremis*" as "A Preface" in *Myth/A Poem*, Iliad Press (2001) and "Why We Alone Live," *Letter Ex* (Oct. 1992).

Manufactured in the United States

First edition

Bigio Morato, an imprint of ARA PACIS PUBLISHERS
Des Plaines, Illinois 60016-1202
www.arapacispublishers.com

Graphic Design by Christine Strohmeyer
Library of Congress Control Number: 2013902785
ISBN: 978-0-9625306-9-2

Contents

Poetry in the Age of Impurity

... after the nocturnal hidden struggle
the more powerful second soul had broken our chains
we awoke crying and it was a sky-blue morning:
like shadows of heroes they sailed:
of the dawn no shadows in the pure silences
of the dawn
in pure thoughts
no shadows
of the dawn no shadows
weeping: we swore our faith to the sky.

Dino Campana

Poetry *in Extremis*

I was perusing through a bookstore once on a visit to New York when I stumbled on the work of a poet who had committed suicide some years earlier. As far back as I could remember, I had always been drawn to the work of writers who had either died indigent, lived under strained circumstances, or in the end took their own lives in some form or another. At that moment, my eyes were suddenly made open to the fact that the truth of our world was only attainable *in extremis* to all the mind-numbing conformity with which it was saddled. I thought of this paradox for a moment, and considered the reasons why I felt this position was so necessary for the poet to assume.

For one, fiercity of perception at the furthest extreme of consciousness is for me a necessary posture if one pretends to the truth. Having built most of our critical theories around decay, hardship, and self-destruction, our culture's fascination with the negative has been for some time playing happy bedfellows with the artist who has perversely recorded every gradation of their own downward spiral like a snowball melting in summer. Still, from my position I see certain patterns, neither metaphors nor blueprints, of victims who have to a certain degree allowed themselves to become martyrs to their own nihilist philosophy, sacrificing themselves on the altar of an indifferent world, their misery safely sanitized for public consumption by an overeager media happy to accommodate the public's taste for a final voyeurism as they fall into the abyss.

Of course, there is another side to the equation, specifically, the reason for creativity's place in our milieu of cultural negation, to the best of my knowledge reduced now to a variety of contradictory ways and means i.e. catharsis, more catharsis, self-immolation, self-absorption, self-mutilation, self-aggrandizement, self-construction, self-reduction, deconstruction, reconstruction, the list of tortures goes on, all pointing to life *in extremis*. Are we to believe any return to classic simplicity possible? This is about as archeologically feasible as the Shroud of Turin, a pale image of some wished-for savior having all the desired features, but staring out under x-ray some poor imitation of divinity that time has rendered a poor joke.

I like the variation of meanings attached to the term *in extremis* — *extrema aeta*, advanced old age, *extrema cauda*, tip of the tail, *extrema linea amare*, to love at a distance, *extrema manus*, final touches, *extremis digitis attingere*, to touch lightly on, to hold tenderly, *extremus ignis*, flickering flame, *in extremo libro secundo*, at the end of the second book, *ad extremum*, at last, at the end. To which does the life of the poet apply, to what truth plied out of the shell, what insight to gain at the tip of the tail, in old age, loving at a distance, rendering final touches, touching lightly so as to hold tenderly the flickering flame at the end of the second book until reaching the end?

There is something in the term that attracts my attention, something that forces me to exist at the extremities, a wish for freedom, a delicate operation to reattain homeostasis. If living *in extremis* to the world is preferable to conformity, it is only because there we find preserved the magic of our muse, the unaltered voice, a refuge from a world of lies and hypocrisy. But how long *in extremis* can we live before falling over the edge of our own sanity? Living on the edge, what greater truth can we drag back to an ever-more indifferent world filled with the poison of its own self-created myth? For all we desire, grappling with the phantom of existence, we are refused our sunlight, denied, made false, never becoming more than false, a battle forced upon us, and who wins? At least from *extremis* we are exempt from hounding blows, we who view our circus dispassionately, harboring our truth from windy heights.

There have been more than enough poets happy to trace the pathetic lines of default and decay that depress our conscience; but there are few who have bravely spoken of their position to the whole issue of self-realization. This becomes more and more important as the world sinks into ever deeper variations of proscribed freedom. The question ultimately becomes one of right position – those who can easily assume one along the edge, those who are but inches from the status quo, those who insist on throwing themselves over the edge to make political or artistic statements. Though they leave the valuation of their legacy in the hands of the very society they could never accept, in all cases, one detects the simple desire for freedom.

But there is another aspect to this drama which involves nothingness as a way of life, or in simpler terms, self-negation assumed for the sake of survival. The only relevant question is – at what price? For some reason, 20th century French thinkers were most astute in articulating answers to this question? They managed, in fact, to devise rather elaborate, but interesting philosophies to explain the human condition. Let's start with the Surrealists, the Existentialists, Sartre and Camus, Baitaille and Leiris, the Deconstructionists and end with the perambulating simulations of Baudrillard. All had their day in the sun, all require explication, but all I believe confront the same intellectual question. Through what elliptical magic of human reasoning can the human mind contrive meaning to a proscribed existence?

Nature is shunned and demoted in all these philosophies because in nature there are no jagged edges, and without the jagged edge no one feels like they are truly living; yet the paradox of living *in extremis* is that for all it provides in stimulation, the feelings it engenders are addictive. Here then the stimulation derived from non-acceptance becomes the vortex around which one's life begins to evolve, until finally the world becomes nothing more than a reflection of one's own construction. For Baudrillard, this is all we have left, but if humanity has distinguished itself in any endeavor it is in its perseverance to find new roads, new avenues to release the spirit.

Da Vinci is said to have regularly bought caged birds in the marketplace merely to set them free, a custom still practiced in Italy mainly by tourists. There is surely here a difference in motive, a difference in meaningful gesture, but we are in truth no longer concerned about such trifles. Freedom now is strictly a commodity, like so many other things in this world taking on increasingly cheaper value. On closer examination, one can even say with regret that freedom is the dullest of lights since we have lost the model; yet occasionally, and with luck, we sometimes find ourselves imbued with the Da Vincian hand, unafraid at least for that moment to release the latch on the door.

Camus stated the dilemma succinctly. There is but one question to answer in order to be at peace with the human condition, that is, whether life is worth living. I believe since life is naturally given us, whether it has external meaning or not, is largely an irrelevant quest. Furthermore, any imposition of meaning via the questing mind automatically negates life's intrinsic meaning. This search for meaning I believe is a reflex to deprivation of human liberty, preventing all from embodying true meaning in unimpeded action.

Since actions are proscribed, how then is it possible for intrinsic meaning to express itself? The answer is that it simply cannot, and as a consequence what exists as human behavior today can only be considered mild to extreme aberrations of countless subjective realities that have no opportunity to calibrate true thoughts to true actions. Instead, we must be afraid of the violent spark, the unexpected blow, a fearful rupture of the human personality, a freakish reflection of internalized fantasies, wished-for contacts with reality, eventual tacit acceptance of whatever exists in the human psyche, aberrational or not. We find it impossible to distinguish between the truly authentic gesture as opposed to the truly false or quirky action or obsessions that are in the final analysis self-destructive and non-integrative.

Now I use the latter term in this sense – that all action is imbued with some underlying, integrative function assisting our wholeness. At almost every level of society one observes countless sacrifices of the essential thing that is us, the repression of true being rendered inoperative out of fear of banishment. Is this not acceptance of an unconscious fatalism, proclaiming we are ultimately unacceptable, an unspoken admittance that we have failed to find our way out of the labyrinth of our own self-engendered – more often than not – self-destructive peculiarities? This is suicide that carries with it a deluge of neuroses and the perpetual reflection of masks, a process thoroughly negating any distinguishing characteristics from the personality save that which is false; yet it is precisely this falsity which is presented to the world as genuine.

The question remains – if all is false, to what are we giving our allegiance? If every philosophy is a compromise for lack of freedom, as Camus suggests, is any philosophy born out of non-freedom truly valid? The question should be – not as Baudrillard suggests how best we can endure abdication of the human experience – but by what means can we retrace our steps to the real? This is the only legitimate question. All others simply beg the question of true existence in what is realistically a false world.

I once believed poetry a means to re-establishing contact with that lost world, a liberating force that could not be stopped once released via the purest language one could grasp, one could decipher, one could discern, one could express. That this language had to be the purest distillation of my true being, that it had to successfully fly beyond the mere representational and live in the purest realm of the experiential, like a tree or flower, that it had to prove itself living without intermediary interpretations to embody the real was axiomatic.

Perhaps this was the great idealism of my youth that had to crash, for today I see poetry as helpless, a record of failed promise, fragments of true being rarified, constructed merely out of "words," not substance, a trail of death that tempts us with life, not true existence or joyous expression pure to itself, but pieces of the whole, like ancient Greek statuary, shattered and broken, that somehow break loose from our repressions, rising before us long enough for us to trace their dying shadows before succumbing to distant echoes and vague memories.

The fragmented pieces of the true self served up to us as art, and their piecing together is the great quest of our time in order to reconstruct a picture of true existence. If the poet lives *in extremis* to what is clearly anathema to true being, then true poetry is possible only if the poet remains pure in body, mind and spirit, for by striking for purity, poetic language must retain it, no longer representing the world, but existent as the world itself.

I was walking with a friend once discussing this issue of purity when he completely discounted the whole notion. "You can't wait for purity!" he said suddenly, angry and frustrated at the whole idea as if mere mention evoked some lost world that was a torment to remember. For the first time in my poetic life I was being forced to eat the disillusionment of the world; yet strangely this exchange catalyzed a new perspective of the disease. If the poet abandoned the notion of purity, what could artistic expression possibly convey? Impurity was the only answer, but had not that, too, become formalized, socially accepted as a way to see the self, an incongruous, unpredictable mixture of the pure and impure? I rejected this ambivalence which left me on the side of mysticism, rooted to love of nature.

Certainly, my insistence on purity was a product of my early environment – growing up on the outskirts of a city, from morning to evening, my first and only view, the sun casting shadows on a forest, denuded, proud, and latent in winter, rising soft, quiet, and inexorable in spring, borne alive to my senses, by its very proximity opening my eyes to the organic nature of existence thrown back to a pantheism long since dead, not only historically, but culturally. Behind me existed another world, the city on a physical line of demarcation.

There was no mystery to my poetic life, but there was in deciphering the fractured myths of an impure world engulfed in maniacal desire to destroy the barest trace of freedom. Purity, of course, a nonexistent luxury reserved only for those intent on remaining close to their own skin. As for my friend, he could not wait for purity, but eventually found nature again, claiming not many years before his death that true knowledge could only be gained from the naturalist. By then, unfortunately, it was too late, for the blood of the bulls had long since been washed away by the sea.

There came a point in my poetic evolution when I realized the true subject of my work was the *mythos* of existence, not the soul of the world, the latter merely the background before which being played out its dynamic. From here it was only a short step to realizing that, like so many other poets before me, I was firmly fixed inside my own symbolism. That poetry was no longer revelation of the world, but a glorying in a symbiotic relationship, each word a mirror, each object a part of myself, each breath of wind a shared oneness, a perspective so true I heeded but one caution and that was to resist narcissism no matter how seductive.

For me, the truth was more important than self-glorification, but I was still the test-tube of my own philosophy, purity of heart my only redemption, the act of creation only as pure. This was the most important thing to preserve, my most unshakable conviction; yet it made me realize there were but two myths to which a poet could abide. The blood from Cronus' wound fell to earth and gave birth to the Furies, avenging parricide and perjury; but Deucalion, warned by his father Prometheus that Zeus planned to destroy humanity for its sins, built a boat and survived, told by an oracle to cast stones over his shoulder to earth from which would spring a new race of men.

A poet can assume either stance, real or imaginary, for no matter how rarified, the poet brings either renewal or *angst* to the world, his blood's purity *cause celebre* for either the destruction or the building of another. In our time the poet is only meant to bleed, their self-mutilation forced to play center-stage as myth, reducing their wounds to a symbol almost Christ-like. Nonetheless, if there is a way to purify humanity's darkest heart, it can only be done by the poet who, like Deucalion, casts their stones behind without fear of retribution, faithful to the notion of the good, though not speaking of things the way they are – as Aristotle observed – but of that which might come to be.

Perhaps Aristotle's idealism can be gently dismissed as merely idyllic,wholly linked to the past, having little if any connection to the present. Being forced to strive for what has no true existence – ourselves alone, reduced and denuded by the greater forces of a regimented world – we must be forgiven for oversight, since without regaining a normative sense of idealism we cannot I believe retrace those fatal steps back to ourselves. Aristotle clearly states that this new projection – which for us must be the true self – is possible, in his words, by virtue of either the likely or necessary.

Now let us consider poetry's two camps – those who prefer merely photographs of reality, as opposed to those who have, as Pasolini describes them, acquired a state of "desperate vitality." The latter have refused to sacrifice their minds to the body politic; instead, they reflect wholly the experiential, disdaining self-consciousness, intent on revealing the true world of existence that has been stolen and repressed, outcasts in a world that revels in duplicity. Others are content to mirror all the pathetic distortions of the human personality, while others resist, clinging to reason, hoping to pull themselves and the consciousness of the world to a higher peak of safety, if they can survive the altitude.

Somehow the question of why we live has come to supersede the question of how, the latter question having become infinitely more important than the former. To ask the question why continually reflects the *angst* of a denuded life of true identity, a by-product of living a proscribed life. The question of how presupposes we are truly living, but are intent on achieving the qualitative. The choice – as usual – is one of *extremis*, but one which shows clearly the true cost of living.

Note how I fall into an instinctive idealism that yearns for a correspondent face to reality. I am the fool who perpetually clings to a failing universe without a shred of evidence true existence can ever be reached as a cultural reality, writing in hope of reconstructing a new model of existence. Must the model conform to my image? As far as my hand can extend. Can this fragmented world of the self even be found, reconstructed, liberated from useless societal strictures?

Among the British Museum's collection of ancient Greek statuary is a truly awe-inspiring piece of shattered sculpture, a torso of a horse *sans* head, mane, and legs. Even with nearly all its parts missing, it speaks clearly of the whole, undeniably present, absent, haunting, powerful, invisible legs and hindquarters, thrashing the earth with their power. Maybe there is death under its hooves, perhaps glory before death, eternal, present, unstoppable, but the part speaks of the whole.

In contrast to the ancients, we choose to engage in endless cultural necrophilia, purposeful rape and disassemblement of popular images to find ultimately nothing of substance. Pasolini said the first quality of any science is to be prophetic, and this I believe is the direction poetic impulse has to take given modern indifference to Aristotle's dictum which is at its base an urging for precisely that. You cannot have a new reality without vision or a grasp of the real; at the same time, you cannot have the real without the power of vision; and since the latter is a wholly abstract entity, one must conclude that empirical precision, when it comes to poetry, is in the final analysis the true goal of poetry achieved as prophecy.

Finally, we should recognize that at best we can only reassemble true being out of the coherent pieces left us from our travails in an unfree world. If we can, however, achieve greater than normal cohesion, perhaps *in extremis* we have a chance for survival provided we retain a grip on true being. As long as we persist in self-denial, we will forever perpetuate the lie that is modern culture, since it simply reflects the lie of all that is false and ignoble in the human heart.

The Imperative

Freedom is that essential space out of which all new form, all newly synthesized truth comes into existence; it is the shadow from which all love emerges, and with it love of all things; it is by its very nature cleansing and purifying; in its essentiality the spark that brings the poem to its highest possible expression both in form and content, clarifying moral and ethical considerations by automatically leading the poet to a more harmonious state of mind which, if sustained, cannot be corrupted. This incorruptible state of mind is the true setting out of which the vital processes of the creative act fulfills its ideal function. That which we see is not polluted by interpretation; those series of impressions which have reached fruition coalesce and integrate; and a synthesis of understanding through ideation the outcome.

Thus, a movement toward truth is implicit to perception reborn as poetic expression. I emphasize freedom in the purest physical and spiritual sense of the word as action follows thought, judgment follows perception, in the most total sense wherein there is complete non-interference in all human action and thought. Any legislation to limit or define freedom in any way has no real jurisdiction, since the condition ultimately cannot be privileged – it is a living reality limited only by force or coercion.

And yet a poet's sense of physical and spiritual wholeness is directly related to how their intuitional and emotional forces are reconciled with the empirical foundations of the creative process. It is at this juncture that the rational, or empirical, harmonizes or clashes with the non-rational, the intuitional and emotional. Ironically, in most cases the non-rational forces win, which, exerting a variety of influences on all aspects of the creative process, is the vital factor necessary to dictating the form of the work.

However, if the ultimate poetic goal is to move toward expression of truth, the poet cannot be limited by empiricism. Eventually the poet must recognize that as they move closer to reality, they move closer to a profounder metaphysical conception of their own being. From this point forward they become a tool of their own making, a probing instrument by which they must measure – in the most refined manner – all reality from a highly intuitionally evolved and purified subjectivity. This methodology eventually transforms into an even greater refined intuitional sense, the true domain of the poet arriving at their metaphysics in means and values from the empirical; and once firmly rooted, their method of logic and discernment becoming purely intuitional, and through a natural balance of means, establishes the psychology of their modus operandi.

Like ever-expanding and intersecting lines, a new level of perception is reached, a newer, more inclusive integration of thoughts and impressions seek higher expression; and the act of creation becomes the means through which the future becomes a possibility. From here, the poet enters the realm of idealism, pursuing that which is most perfect in reality. If followed to its logical end,this is the ultimate result of the creative process. Like branches,the pursuit extends and permeates the life of the poet, bringing them ever newer interest in reality and the quality of their own existence; in effect, it allows them to key into more progressive modes of thinking, allowing them to seek ever higher artistic form.

But psychological barriers and technical advances have forced the poet to rearrange their senses at oblique angles to the world. One can readily see a direct relationship between the increase of political authoritarianism in the world and a correspondent increase in the internalization of the poet's response to reality. At the same time, there has been gradual distortions of the creative process. The result has been a violent rejection of external reality, or acknowledgement of any objectively discernible natural process by which to measure the value or validity of any artistic expression as well as a complete loss of idealism.

This shift to purely subjective frames of reference is in direct conflict with the biological realities in us and surrounding us which, if left free, are forever moving toward balance, harmony, and reconciliation with nature. To correct the imbalance, to give back the creative process its rightful dynamic, the poet of today must continually answer and reanswer this question. To what condition can we attribute the realization of harmony and unify?

It should be evident I am drawing a critical relationship between freedom and a natural movement toward harmony and reconciliation with reality; while any lack of freedom will by necessity incline toward disharmony and conflict. In the formation of poetic consciousness, it is this critical factor which I am concerned most. Without a firmly based awareness of freedom, there can be no true substantial development of the poetical mind and no real comprehension of the unity of all natural processes. The creative process is perhaps the most evident display of nature's tendency toward harmony; for even if the poet exists in a state of disharmony, poetry as a means of clarification is indicative of a desire to reach unity of being whether the poet is conscious of it or not. That unity of being is the ultimate objective, not the poem which – at the risk of redundancy – is only a reflection of the poet's physical and spiritual wholeness.

Every artistic manifesto written in the 20th century that proposed a new, creative process was only a repositioning of mentality to fit the social expectations of the time. Generally, they offered no renewed faith or understanding of natural process, only ingratiating salutes to socialist-realism. What true poetic integration was achieved? The result was merely objectified neurosis and fragmentation, though it is not accurate to say the extremism of our age has not brought insight. Picasso – deliberately or inadvertently – showed us something of the changed character of the 20th century mind, though we cannot logically go back to an earlier, less configured age. Nature remains the same no matter how eloquent Picasso was in his rejection of it.

Still, the cultural sensibilities of a classical Greece, the Renaissance, or the Romantic era of the 19th century are, admittedly, of no influence on today's modern society as are none of the arts in general created out of our own cultural milieu. What is important to realize is that the poet cannot return to the past nor emulate it in such a way that a new vision becomes impossible. On the other hand, neither can the poet exist very long in the vacuity of our age without incorporating the best of the past into the best of what can exist tomorrow.

In explaining the nature of Zen painting, Eugen Herrigal describes what I believe the highest possible achievement of poetic form. His description refers to the visual effect of Zen painting, but he articulates what I think is the true test of pure poetry from the perspective of effect and form. Not only does perspective become pointless and disappears, explains Herrigal, but the relation of observer to observed is thoroughly eliminated. Space surrounds the observer who stands in the center without being the center and is at one with "the heartbeat of things."

In effect, what this description illustrates is a wholistic view of the world no longer taking on a fragmented appearance because it is organically perceived. Theoretically, this should be the entire psychological effect of any artistic form, since art – whether harmonious or disharmonious in form – tends toward unity of design, if not in rendering, at least presupposed in the very process of its creation. Whatever unifying order is missing from the work is brought to it by the artist, even if the work is formalistically disordered and deliberately contrived.

This achievement in wholistic form can only be understood if we look at creativity as an absolute reflection of the artist's interior life; that if purified tends to reflect a wholeness and completeness dependent and reflective of the inner purity and completeness of the creator. Form need no longer deliberately strive to express idea, but rather allowed into existence, and by so doing, reflect the simple oneness of nature and the position therein we hold. By discarding a mechanistic view of the creative process, we are finally revealing the truer form beneath the surface of our own perceptions and those which must be psychologically forever coming into existence, discarding certain trained, formalized responses to the creative imagination in the process.

This perspective leads us away from a reconciliation with matter and reality as we perceive it. It makes very clear the separate, but distinct inter-dependent worlds of being and reality at work at various levels of the creative process. If nothing more, modernist art has shown the advantages and disadvantages of such a fragmented approach to creativity and its formalization within various artistic disciplines.

Nevertheless, there could be no continually true significance to art or its content if form did not evolve at the same time as the ideational synthesis within the artist. It is only logical to assume that in order to express any broadened understanding of reality and all its processes, form must adapt to need expressly demanded as the urgency of thought continuously brings a manifestation of itself as a reality into the living world. To really see a thing we must adjust our visual apparatus. If the adjustment is adequate, the thing is seen indistinctly or not all as illustrated by the following description by Oretga of a garden seen through a window.

"Looking at the garden, we adjust our eyes in such a way that the ray of vision travels through the pane without delay and rests on the shrubs and flowers. Since we are focusing on the garden and our ray of vision is directed toward it, we do not see the window but look clear through it. The purer the glass the less we see it. But we can also deliberately disregard the garden and, withdrawing the ray of vision, detain it at the window. We then lose sight of the garden; what we still behold of it is a confused mass of color which appears pasted to the pane. Hence to see the garden and to see the window pane are two incompatible operations which exclude one another because they require different adjustments."

In reality the two adjustments do not exclude each, for we are still cognizant of the garden's existence, that is, the object of our attention, though our perception may adjust itself to see only the pane. In effect, the reality of the pane as the medium functions as the means or form through which we ultimately see the object of our concentration. This whole process in actuality is really saying more about the inborn capacities of human consciousness; that is, the ability to zero in on any object or idea that fills our range of attention, while at the same time mentally maintaining vital points of reference for all previously perceived and recognized realities via memory and/or visual ideation. From a poetic point of view, the reconciliation of these various adjustments of perception are essential for any real synthesis of thought and form.

Ernest Cassirer pin-points this distinction between such visual adjustments, but from the essential perspective of human phenomenology. "I have in mind simultaneously the object to which I am reacting at the moment and the one to which I am going to react," he writes. "One is in the foreground, the other in the background. But it is essential that the object in the background be there as a possible object for future reaction. Only thus can I change from one to the other. This presupposes the capacity for approaching things only imagined, possible things, things which are not given in the concrete situation."

That capacity for approaching things that are "imagined possible things" is the very key to all continual synthesis inherent to the creative process; it is precisely that which is fundamentally possible of things which make the dynamic of poetry a living reality, giving content dimension and meaning to poetic creation. If poetry is devoid of meaning, it is only because of the absence of a true synthesis of mind, heart, and logic. Often form is subordinated to what is socially accepted, further reducing poetry to the dangerous level of mere social utilitarianism.

This is quite evident when one considers that the majority of artistic creations of any age usually share some attitudinal as well as formalized artistic agreement with the society out of which they are born. This, however, does not discount the vision of the poet or their need to continually express a new, formalized concept of the world; in fact, it is almost required the poet maintain this instinct in order to survive at all as an artist.

In the end, the creative process is not simply one of action and reaction; it is not mechanistic, but at its heart truly at variance with the basically contrived and psychologically mechanistic modern age. This is why the modernist arts have nothing to say about freedom or what can exist tomorrow, since today's artist rather tacitly accepts the general state of the modern world. Only the poet who truly liberates themselves from the misconceptions of their time can ever hope to achieve integration of being which dictates the fluidity of poetic expression. Only when the poet is free can they observe the organic unity of nature and truly understand Heraclitus' admonition – "They are at variance with that which they are in most continual association."

Hence, the creative process knows no collective identity, only in the accretion of knowledge, poetic synthesis, and complementarity of endeavor. Only in the freedom to follow the creative process does one begin to see the synergistic end it pursues, the poetic truth it longs to affirm by agreement with other minds. It is the symbol from which true, philosophical enlightenment is finally gained and clarity of vision becomes possible. It is to wait, to be patient, to respond at the right moment without forcing the work at hand, to know instinctively the poem is being born at the right moment in time; that all things move toward synchronization. It veers from pain or self-conscious effort if the poet has reached a certain level of self-liberation. It resolves the stress of emotional and intellectual compromise with a world saturated in a socialist ethos because it implies no politic beyond the dynamic of the individual.

The creative process is the only means by which the poet's metaphysics can actually balance and consequently give birth to new meaning, the poet's metaphysics merely the mirror image of the empirical universe. In order for poetic expression to truly reflect the real face of humanity, an exact balance must be struck between what exists in reality and its value revealed. Only with complete freedom to explore the human condition without interference or censorship by either subtle or overt coercion can this ever be reality.

This objective has always been the idealistic expectations of poetry from the beginning — to bring humanity together and fuse it in perfect harmony, to awaken society at large to symbols they are unable to articulate, but once done, activating its stagnancy with a renewed idealism of form. We are then brought to an expanded perspective of perceptual reality. In this respect, the reduction to subjective frames of reference releases the potential of affirming new form and its inter-connectivity with substance.

Unfortunately, this has not been the cultural goal of our time. Instead, we are buried in useless poetic and societal debris, symbols and archetypes that have no real relation to the true nature of reality. At the same time, if there is to be a true revision of modern poetics, it must begin with a new introspection based solely on the real realities of being, the real realities of world. If to truly measure the efficacy of poetry and all art as an active reflection of reality and ever-evolving truth; if to study art is to be ultimately led back to the character of the creator, we must focus on the creative process. For therein lies the key to judging the quality of expression, refinement of purpose, balance, and genuineness of impulse that initiates the work. We must go back to the beginning point, or at least the most logical and immediately perceived to find our proper bearings again. This involves a reexamination of the creative process if we are to advance culturally again in the highest sense; that is, to know the means through which a higher understanding of ourselves can be realized.

Without a basic awareness of freedom, there can be no real, logical interpretation of the senses, no logical development of being on which rests the quality of poetic expression. Furthermore, without a firm grounding on this essential principle, there can be no real insight, no poetic expression without doubt, no hope for resolution of paradox or conflict. The age has too radically changed, the demands for higher understanding too urgent. Snapshots of reality are not enough; yet the creative process is the one, vital aspect of human psychology that offers the momentum needed to rid ourselves of archaism and authoritarianism in all forms, capable of giving us glimpses of what can be, if we meet the challenge of personal liberty without the medieval, ignorant fear of chaos.

If we are to gradually return to a belief in transformation, freedom can no longer be considered merely a philosophical term to be debated; nor can the creative process be viewed merely as the disjointed catharsis of human stress, agony, and confusion. It may be that in order to refind purity of consciousness, the poet must temporarily retreat into that sanctuary of being where integrity cannot be assaulted. From there it is possible to view oneself against the context of the civilized world in which we live; and by so doing establish a new context of being merely by opposition to it. In fact, if this is not done, there can be no refinement or purification of the creative process in our time.

This strain of isolation becomes the trial from which emerges a true sociability with the world, silence of being the arena out of which immaturity and self-delusion are revealed. Finally exposed to one's own scrutiny, the poet can evolve a sound, poetic sensibility without outracing any limits of character. It is this kind of extreme isolation that, although unnatural, is necessary I believe to find freedom and the creative process intact. In really no other circumstance can the poet hope to establish not only a new poetic method, but the character necessary to survive the corruption of the age. To live in order to flower – that is the final imperative.

A Room in Brindisi

Sun. 16 Sep 2012

I can't tell you how much I admire and respect you for submitting to the unrelenting poetic muse that will, of course, not drive you completely mad, but will open doors of perception and blind you for a time to everything else. But it's the kind of madness that dictates its own logic and allows one to live the truth of one's own existence. Your poems become evidence after the fact, and the truest, most powerful poems come out of those moments of inner transformation you seize and articulate. It is those moments you have to recognize.

Now the inner transformation of being I'm referring to is beyond reason, which means your poetic language will always seek its own form. This is what I mean when I say all poetic truth rises from the subconscious. The art, shall we say, is giving shape to a distinct language rising from below. The true test is the poet's ability to hear the voice. The language may sound irrational, but your goal as the poet is to free it from itself. Everything poetic then is after the fact, not forced, not formulated. This is the poetic language you seek, the purity of your own voice beyond the detritus of the lived experience. All human truth rises to purity and in all the purity of language you retain and reshape in the light of the real world. And is not the real world, inner and outer, what we all seek to articulate in natural poetic language that not only affirms living truth, but achieves its highest expression as beauty?

I cannot say it better than Heraclitus– "That which is in opposition is in concert, and from things that differ comes the most beautiful harmony ... The hidden harmony is stronger than the visible ... How could anyone hide from that which never sets?"

Your work is so very close. I hear the voice, then it falls away into linear lines, then it comes back again. Think the gain, not the loss. Strip away what obscures the light and the dark and you will witness the resolution of the paradox.

The following are fragmentary notes I made after several months of intense dream analysis in the early spring of 1992. I am not certain any of these fragments can fully explain the profound transformation I underwent at the time. Perception changes, ideas alter, some retained, others discarded, but all eventually transfigure into a further variation on what I believe to be at the heart of the human experience, the paradox of life and death.

Through true being true existence is expressed, yet the only way we can know true being is through direct, intuitive knowledge of desire. The greater self-repression, the greater the impossibility of direct, intuitive knowledge. The greater preponderance of consciousness, the less contact with true existence. The mistake has been to believe true being resides in consciousness alone when, in fact, true being resides in the unconscious. To know then true existence, consciousness must satisfy the promptings of the unconscious.

Since we must accept the world as a failure, we must accept the fact that true being has been murdered, that the modern soul is partially if not completely dead, creating a dread of realizing true existence. This feeling is at cross purposes with the true nature of being which is of itself endless, timeless and paradoxically linked to death in that death is a reality equally endless, equally timeless. The human experience clearly shows that being, like time, is endless. To consciousness, any limitation suggests wholly and exclusively death; thus, to realize true being is to struggle with the erroneous conception that to exist is to die.

If the link between true being and death has been forged, distortion becomes the mirror through which existence is perceived and harmony becomes a false reflection of being. The only way to free oneself is to realize the association. At that point one confronts the true existential condition by direct knowledge of being, direct knowledge of death, a feeling of having reached the end, an embrace of death as the only way to resolve the question of true existence. In the end, the tenuous survival of true being depends on love. Deprivation destroys true existence coming first in the form of social conformity, then through various forms of social repression, until reaching the final stage of complete self-repression.

Freud recognized the unconscious, but claimed it had no logic, no other existence than blind lust, the id, the libido being the presumable mad seat of the unconscious. He failed to see the unconscious as the source of true existence. The imagery of the Surrealists revealed the unconscious trying to achieve harmony with the real world and how completely out of touch it was with its own existence. But they made the mistake of formalizing the suffering, disharmonious voice they had liberated. They saw the seat of true existence in the unconscious, the oracular voice of true art, true being, true spirit, but were unable to understand the distortions that poured out of them as art, as though vehicles of all the madness caused by centuries of social repression.

What they failed to realize was the full impact of their psychological discovery. Touching on true existence, they assumed its nature one of disorder, so in formalizing disorder, they articulated not the inherent order and harmony of being, but its pain and fears. They assumed this was the true nature of being. Other than the artificial formalism of the society in which they were surrounded, they finally were left with nothing, not even the satisfaction of having expressed true being.

All that exists today is the artificial order of organized society, the dominance of will and consciousness, alongside our formalizations of consciously ordered structures of religious orders and institutions which, rather than respecting the individual, negates true existence via collectivization, keeping humanity perpetually outer-directed. Words like, "The mind is stronger than the body," or "The will can conquer" are simply misnomers. Since life is lived mostly out of will, or consciousness, we cannot possibly be acting out of the purity of true being. The term "human being" expresses exactly the nature of true existence.

True being is not found but revealed in glimpses throughout life via art, the body, via sex when sex touches the whole being. There is no direct, conscious road to knowledge of true existence. It can only be verified experientially. No intellectual process working backward can articulate what is wholly unconscious in nature. As long as humanity can be kept away from hearing the voice of true being, each individual as unique entity is eventually made dead in the profoundest sense of the term.

If we can believe the nature of Christianity as expressed in the symbolic acts of Jesus, the ability to breathe life into the dead is reserved only for those in complete touch with true being. Death in its living human form breeds more death, each generation thwarted from reaching true existence. If we can hear the pain of repressed being, death's contradictory nature can be resolved by full conscious expression of being.

To a great extent one must decide to let go, risking death to resolve the paradox. It finally becomes a play of opposites, a resolution by itself of the paradox of life as opposed to death. Whatever theories of duality, these would resolve themselves if given absolute freedom of play. Unfortunately, modern culture is not based on the full play of human liberty; consequently, we are forced to maneuver backward and forward, until we have achieved so-called "true being" or "true existence" as defined by a corrupt culture. The effects of interference and deprivation have taken on social forms all their own and accepted as the true face of true existence. Without courage to meet the paradox, there can be no life and no real death, only an ongoing tension between the two until death as a fact ends the neurotic issue.

Fear of death is a perversion of true being which is limitless *in potentia*. Death resolves itself since it is dual-natured, that is, limitless as being and existence continuously reborn in humanity through birth of species and at the same time limited by the natural course of human existence. But it is not possible to eliminate death in all forms; it is a reality of the physical world and is dual-natured and limitless. This dual nature must be understood if we are to understand the relationship between the unconscious and the functions of consciousness and the former's place and purpose in the real world.

Under these psychological circumstances, the experience of the full existential dilemma will be felt for what it is as meaninglessness, nothingness, emptiness. We fail to realize that true being, as seated in the unconscious, is the source not of emptiness, but of fullness and order. As long as we search outside ourselves we are ultimately doomed to fail in understanding our place in nature. Without understanding how the dichotomy between mind and body, consciousness and the unconscious came about, we are doomed to live death in living form, until death as a physiologic truth claims us. Without fear, there is no existentialist dilemma, no God in the theological sense of the term, only true existence via true being.

Why We Alone Live

Modern revolutions have all the earmarks of romanticism, but their real character invariably is one of violence. The gunshots create wounds, the wounds bleed, life ebbs away. The actual face of revolution is one so corrupted by ignorance, lies, distrust, and propaganda, it can never escape its materialistic intent, power for power, victim for victim. One revolution is forced through by another in a rapid exchange of conflicting wills and rhetoric. "It disperses and gathers," said Heraclitus. "To those entering the same river, other and still other waters flow."

In literature, revolutionary intent is not unusual. The chant can be strong, perhaps in all poets in every time frame. But to what end and for what effective purpose? Words, merely words, symbols representing ideas, and ideas leading to action, but action, nonetheless.

Words, symbols, power – they marry interchangeably in strange rituals, but in the end it is always the same – the order tighter, the graves deeper, the rhetoric more tiringly redundant. If we perceive the existence of any true revolutionary force in the poet it is only at the moment they break from the resistance of their social image into the unpretentious action of the heart. They are onlookers peering over the barricades, clutching their notebooks ever fast, quite aware of the difference between contemplation and action. But the world offers them but two choices, the gun or the idea. They must choose between the two, while the many are sucked into the maelstrom of modern, political thinking, and therein poetic thinking is utterly destroyed.

The true poet knows politics is primitive; it bases its existence on the inter-dependence, not the independence of the human mind. Between the poet's own individual drama and the brawn of violence, in eagerness for social change, their voice is drowned by the mercilessness of a nuclear warhead grinning in its hangar. Still every poet believes their work will respond to the ideal of pure freedom. They never let go this hope, and their work invariably responds to this urging in some way. Consequently, their dream is that their work will contribute to this collective ideal which civilization has yet to realize.

The modern age prides itself on its ability to dissect, interpret, analyze and categorize its artistic products. We want to see and experience history before our very eyes, before the corpse is cold, the word dry, the author dead. There is a neurotic compulsion to chronicle the barest movement, the most obvious lurch, the faintest vibration of modern life. We will not, simply put, let the world exist as a floating hope in the human mind. We are, as a consequence, anachronisms of our own consciousness.

Many poets have absorbed this self-conscious attitude. They assume it in their work, and naturally their work reflects a great degree of imitation, restraint, dullness, esoteric predictions, and flaccid maxims useful only for academia. Time reduced poetry to an exercise in Pavlovian psychology, indulged in to merely create response without a shred of genuineness either in style or content. If the poet fails to live up to any self-ordained ideals of perfection, they usually become second-rate political minds, content portraying the individual drama as subservient to political forces. Denying the personal, they expose nothing more in their work than broken dreams and failed potential, incapable of rising above any and all polarizing forces.

It is also absurd to think the nature of poetic consciousness has not changed as radically as the modern world, perhaps more; yet now there is a greater need than ever to recontemplate natural phenomena, to transform that reawareness into a new, conceptual understanding of future possibilities. Like a wave or a sun unspokenly regarded, the poet rediscovers them within all their purity.

The poet must be exceedingly strong, insightful, wise, and compassionate, able to work with their life as though a tool infused with orderly passion and intelligence, revealing the exact curve of a muscle or the exact reality of an emotion. They must become greater than they actually are in order to preserve and rarify their normal self, to actually know themselves. Natural process allows this, the force implicit to social change does not.

As the sun changes dimensions in the poet's hands, so their self-image transforms. This is the other world that splits into fragments and is reassembled by the power of that greater sun, no more to reflect the mundanity of space we inhabit, or the hour we presumably die in disillusionment. The poet must metamorphosize existence, not the existence they already know, but that which we deeply feel.

I look for the poetic example – Mayakovsky, pounding out industrial chants to the Russian revolution, commits suicide. Essenin, who accepted the Revolution in theory, but not the Bolshevik manner, commits suicide. Pasternak and Mandelstam – both hounded, both involved with the exposition of the central point of self within the unsteadiness of social upheaval. Mandelstam dies in a labor camp, leaving behind a collection of poetry appropriately titled *Stone*.

"It is an example of the supreme idiocy of our time that we care more for the preservation of militarism and the mass man than the individual mind." he writes. "More for high-yield, high financed scientific engineering that is seemingly blind to organic unity... The word is flesh and bread. It shares the fate of bread and flesh: suffering. People are hungry. The State is even hungrier... There is nothing hungrier than the contemporary State, and a hungry State is more terrifying than a hungry man. To show compassion for the State which denies the word shall be the contemporary poet's social obligation and heroic feat."

Pasternak was spared the slaughter, but exiled to the silence of his own conscience. "Any artist should expect good from nowhere else but his own imagination," he wrote. "A poet is not an author, but the subject of a lyric, facing the world in the first person."

I imagine a little, glowing fire, hot as flame, burning in their chests, trying perpetually to get at the central meanings put into life, fashioning wings for a wooden bird in the belief it will fly and, of course, it must. That is the fundamental essence of hope and the issue we are all after to solve, spiritual strength bathed in moral direction. That flame is the poet's simultaneity with life. To read Pasternak is to see how this flame struggled to keep afloat in the face of restriction and the threat of sudden death. This is courage poetically diligent; it is in this way the sun becomes the sun again as it was at the beginning, the wave becomes the first that brought the amoeba crawling under the microscope. The eye exists and appreciates mystery again because it has become valued, and its value becomes as bright as the sun itself, nothing regarded as insignificant, until raised high enough and elucidated for the mass of minds straining their necks for a view.

In our modern passion for truth, the sensitive natures are the only ones desperate, capable, and aware enough to take on this poetic risk, that is, articulating the source of all we consider the true, living reality and potentials of the human experience. This is the thread to be tied. We are destinies born from an innate symbolism within ourselves, separate from any meanings that could be attached to us, even nationhood.

We face a struggle to determine our individual destinies rather than a collective one as a nation. A country of circumstance, sometimes we are unexpectedly conscious of the central meaning of our dynamism; yet instead of encouraging us, it frightens us away with its turns and futurity, its speed and struggle to express philosophy.

Could existentialism as a philosophy have taken such a grip on society at large had not there been such despondent feelings within those individuals who had intellectually accepted such self-negation as a very real reality? I believe we have come to a point in history where such dangerous games of self-annihilation are not only obsolete, but need therefore to be challenged and shown to be intellectually bogus by exposing such duplicity on the part of artists and writers who pretend to be enlightened, but are as much victim as the public they successfully dupe with their *angst* disguised as art.

To what more can I be sensitive than to such abdication of self-responsibility and the very act of creation? This can never be acceptable in any age, least of all in ours where the tenuous grip on reality and endless varieties of cultural self-abuse have taken hold and have become all but institutional in their permanence in the modern West.

It goes without saying that to expose one's image to the public is to take responsibility for the image projected. The truth of the matter is once the image is fully observable, it is possible for it to represent one of total opposition to the real self. This is an unjustified fear. Better to accept whatever image one projects, whether it be accepted by the public or not. The difference between those who accept the direction their image takes and those who do not depends on the nature of the image itself whether be true or false.

Poetic failure is in truth the outer manifestation of our human failure, our reluctance or inability to express the deeply apparent reasons for our own existence, why we alone live, love, sense, act, destroy, dream, hope, breathe or exist before beauty, ugliness, sincerity or lies. This existential confrontation is enough to show the naive insufficiency of any political definition of art.

If the poet's work is true, real, intense, full of risk, daring, intelligence, sensitivity, everything into which they have worked to put meaning, it cannot fail to reflect a similar mind and heart in others. Above all else, nothing can wipe away the poet's essential humanness or similarity of both emotional and intellectual experience with others. If they are sensitive and brave enough to express their evolution, to free themselves from all restraints of the past, to look carefully over the shaded places, the days and nights of change in their face and the faces of all others, we will finally as a civilization advance into the munificence of an apolitical reality. Only then will we truly see what is trying to manifest itself as a reality in the context of what we understand as civilized life.

On the Difficulties of Poetry in Translation

If contemporary poetry cries for a viable critical hearing on the landscape of American letters, poetry in translation languishes like an abandoned child at its outer fringes. And although ruled by a sympathetic, but indifferent *cognoscenti*, one sees a cultural centrism ingrained that is almost impregnable. In spite of our pluralistic makeup as a nation, the poetic achievements of other countries has exerted at best a negligible impact on American poetry, though it should be obvious to even the dullest of cultural observers that many if not all of our cultural traditions have their roots elsewhere in the world.

A compelling example of such cultural transference are Charles Baudelaire's translations into French of the works of Edgar Allan Poe in the 19th century, perhaps one of the few instances in literary history whereby an American poet's cultural identity was successfully transposed into a distinctly

French cultural light, so much so that one can almost claim a kind of miraculous victory for Baudelaire who understood the cultural issues at stake undertaking such an act of transference. His interest in the Gothic tradition of the English language provided just such impetus behind his effective renderings of the errant American writer. One might even say that because of Baudelaire's efforts, French literature became more French than American, for in effect the French poet had successfully made Poe one of their own.

It seems to me then in order to really talk about the quality of poetry in translation one has to really navigate the treacherous waters of cultural signification to get at its value; that poetry in translation, albeit high-mindedly rendered at least in theory, cannot be judged but by two standards i.e. its ability to transmute the human experience into a living reality for the foreign reader, and secondly to recreate the authenticity of language whereby the translator becomes in the words of one literary critic, "an inheritor and transcender... an opener of new spaces." For me, these new spaces require the cognizance of a translator willing to reach beyond the formalized meaning of words to achieve the goal of poetic transference that fully communicates the living experience to the reader. One could say the ideal best translator of poetry is to ultimately erase the linguistic gap that necessarily exists between two cultures.

The truth is that poetry in translation is an attempt to radicalize foreign poetic expression into a newly minted language, in spite of the fact these translations exist far from the cultural context of the poet undergoing transition. Nevertheless, they remain by sheer circumstance alien works to all, though gathering in the process often long histories of translators behind them, and equally long, sometimes illustrious pedigrees of patrons and devotees who have struggled to make a foreign poet's work better known. But in reality, poetry in translation in the Western tradition has largely become a game of literary revisionism, at worst, the self-indulgence of the translator, at its best, a serious attempt to bridge cultural and linguistic gaps to better understand and appreciate the artistic heritage of another country's humanist perspective.

What is really lost in translated poetry, however, is not so much fidelity to the original language, even in the most stylized and creative approximations, but its artistic and intellectual impact as a living contextual reality of the human experience. What is often derived instead are skeletal peculiarities into which the translator fills in the imagined features, much in the same manner a forensic scientist reconstructs the features of a lost Neanderthal. For the sake of the imagination, we imagine the approximation of features like the original hominid, but in point of fact we are approximating the imagination more than gaining some idea of the skeleton's soul. Is this really a question of fidelity to the translated language, or are these poetic reconfigurations of the original simply idiosyncratic excursions into the world of approximations and as such must be recognized as having a life distinctly their own?

I think the real impotence of poetry in translation today lies in its utter lack of impact on the literary culture at large, particularly in the West. This may partly be due to the fact that poetry in translation accounts for less than 1% of the total number of books published. It has become more an endeavor of dilettantism and publisher prestige than an event of actual literary importance, in spite of our continual praises to multiculturalism. This in publishing terms may simply mean that we care little, if at all, about the literature of other countries more than presenting literary faces that merely reinforce our delusion of having achieved a worldly face of our own.

A young university student from Bologna I met on a train going to Rome from Florence was shocked to know that I had even heard, much less read the work of Italian poets like Eugenio Montale and Dino Campana. Likewise, an equally surprised Russian student thought it remarkable that I knew anything about the poetry of Osip Mandelstam and Mayakovsky. Here in the United States, it is a challenge to find college undergraduates with even glancing familiarity with Walt Whitman, probably the most quintessential American poet, let alone the literary lights of other countries.

Thus, the difficulty in assessing some critical value to poetry in translation is the difficulty of establishing more definitively what criteria to use to judge its ultimate poetic value. Is it poetry in its own right, or poetry as near an approximation of the true language of the poet under translation? Susan Sontag points out three basic approaches: translation by explanation, translation by adoption, and translation by improvement. All of these methodologies, of course, assume some radical engagement of the work at some deeper level of linguistic and cultural contact, though they propose no small challenge to finding the fairest point of departure for making sound critical appraisals. The best translations may, in fact, be ones wholly predicated on taste alone, similar to distinguishing the best bouquet of certain wines, if we assume the authenticity of the language is circumspect.

But this cultivated sense is not easily achieved, the effects eventually become predictable, and the poetry under translation very often lost or ineffectual. Unfortunately, this has become the only debatable issue related to assessing the quality and importance of most poetry in translation. As Ilan Stavans accurately points out, "Translation is a Quixotic endeavor: an impossible quest. Every translator seeks to create a 'perfect' counterpart to the original, but perfection is not a human quality. And so the process itself is doomed from the start....In that sense, the translator is a parasite of sorts: he eats from someone else's food. But he also allows the artist to flourish, to be free from his own cultural and linguistic imprisonment, and in this sense he is a liberator."

One could make the point that every poet writing in the world today, whether in the sphere of the West, or at every corner of the Third World is challenged by their own cultural and linguistic heritage, and that to a certain extent Stavans' claim that the translator acts as liberator to their work is wholly accurate. But one might ask for whom and from what is the poet being liberated? Poetry does not affect the culture any longer in ways that it once did in a more agrarian, less easily communicable times when the telephone, computer, fax, the extremely advanced technology of book production were simply not there to be exploited. The poet has become but a lost voice on the horizon, a cultural presence and prophetic voice we imagine still exists, but is not really near at hand. Poetry's universality has been calibrated to secular voices of class, race, or gender, not the shared human experience, and it is precisely this shared human experience which I believe ultimately defines the best intentions of poetry in translation.

But more than that I believe the best poetry in translation at heart attempts to retrace steps back to that authenticity of voice and experience that lies at the core of all lived experience. In essence, its success lies in its efforts to remake this authenticity into a living voice, not an artificial one that takes liberties to evoke the poetic texture of the language. I think the best poetry in translation strives for fidelity to literal meaning, and by so doing allows the voice and persona to become a living identity within the body of the new language. By so doing, one can hardly argue for tampering with the original language in question, yet at the same time giving felicity and consideration to the poetic evocations brought to the fore by rendering such fidelity to the poet's view of reality and all that can be related to it beyond the translator's own cultural touch points. As translator Eliot Weinberger points out, "Poetry is not what gets lost in translation; poetry is that which is worth translating. The untranslatable poem is simply one which has not yet found its translator."

The assumption is that the best translations of poetry are done by poets who theoretically possess such mastery. However, with today's decided absence of any aesthetic concern with language, what one gets, instead, are largely prose versions of poetry that read more like transcriptions than poetry shaped out of the very architecture of the translator's native tongue. The reason why may be the tremendous gap between classic traditional poetry written in English and the anti-aesthetic attitude toward art in general.

I believe this anti-aesthetic attitude has not left poetry untouched and may have in many ways degraded poetic expression to the point of creating its own self-negation as a distinctive form of art. The concern for line, rhythm, assonance, and form – among many other features related to content, theme, meaning and metaphor—is to a large extent missing from contemporary poetry, and with it has come a rather passionless approach toward poetry in translation.

Clearly, the best poetry in translation must find the best literal meaning in the best choice of words, yet at the same time provide the sound that makes sense aesthetically. The worst poetry in translation attempts to reconstruct the aesthetics of a foreign language, even worse to attempt a recreation of the poetic ambiance of the work in question. This is really equivalent to trying to recreate the experience of standing at the top of the Himalayas in the middle of the Gobi desert. By no stretch of the imagination can the experience can be duplicated much less successfully simulated.

As Baudrillard accurately pointed out, these very simulations have become the very substantive forms of the culture impossible to escape, creating their own set of precepts and paradigms applicable in the practice of nearly every artistic pursuit, including the art of poetry in translation. And it is precisely because of this challenge to poetic authenticity that poetry in translation either rises or falls to its level of relevancy to the culture at large.

The Fate of the Word

One day on examination of the 20th century's contribution to philosophical thought, we may finally recognize our self-proclaimed brilliance of modernist ideas were merely exercises in form; but in the absurdity of such reductionism we may also find ourselves faced with the real challenge of discerning anew the intelligible laws of the universe as embodied in the poetic word inspired by reason, reveling in the power of an inspired language set as a balancing rod between humanity and the world, profoundly changing the very fabric of civilization, returning us to faith in being and our real place in the matrix of nature.

The poetic word carries the immense responsibility of time, knowledge and meaning; it is the embodiment of all we are and all we will ever mean; it takes the final hour of illumination and transforms it into another more brilliant, more variegated than any that preceded it; it ties together the beginning and the end of each segmented portion of reality we view separate from the greater element, showing us unity of design as well as corruption of substance.

"The Law (the Logos) is as here explained," writes Heraclitus, "but men are always incapable of understanding it, both before they hear it, and when they have heard it for the first time. For all things come into being in accordance with this Law, men seem as if they had never met with it, when they meet with words and actions such as I expound, separating each thing according to its nature and explaining how it is made."

For Heraclitus, human nature has no power of understanding, except through articulation of divine nature, that faculty that separates us from the dogmatism of linear thinking as opposed to implicit trust of the prophesying word. He realized the significance of the Sibyl who "with raving mouth uttering her unlaughing, unadorned, unincensed words reaches out over a thousand years with her voice, through the (inspiration of the) god."

The modern world buries this infinite, psychic, poetic drama as fast as it can in fear of its transformative power over humanity's conscience; but it can never be extinguished, even though the poetic word as ever-evolving, integrative symbol has been relegated to obscurity where its meaning, its very significance is questioned and disclaimed. This psychic, poetic drama is uttered as poetry; and as possessed as the poet may appear, they live the divine nature of the *logo* psychically for reasons which, on a rational level, they may never adequately be able to explain.

Identifying with the true word, the poet endeavors to speak, seeing nothing but their relationship to nature. Whatever they see, their entire creative life is spent seeking out what lies on the other side of their vision. They strain to feel nature's rhythm clearly. To the so-called civilized world, the poet is born blind. They cannot see the world for what it is hiding, purer life, as they strive to understand its meaning. No matter what poetic imagery, they are blind but to one force, that which created them and that which will take them. The word interjects and becomes endowed, the word reinfused, the word in opposition to hatred, disharmony and self-destruction, the word as representative of reality and reflective of our natural propensity to create language, as much reality as any object, but by nature separate.

The real question is how the word-as-*logo*, as metaphor, as representation of reality, extends, interrelates and explains the vastness of being and the nature of the world. Poetry exploits the mytho-poetic qualities of words because it alone witnesses the marriage of reality to symbol and symbol to reality. At its highest, integrated transcendence it realizes the world as one, reconciling disparity, all the time cognizant of the primary unity of the cosmos. Ideally, poetry at its purest, evocative power partakes of an organic symbolism born of the fusion of words at the deepest level of being. It is in this primal, emotive and intuitional sphere that the *logo*, the word as representative of the basic order of the universe, multiples and is born symbol.

In this respect, there is no doubt that linguistically words exist as a catalyzing agent of the psyche. The logic of words, especially those which embody the greatest understanding of reality, automatically have an illuminative and tranquilizing effect on the individual, for by nature they ultimately absorb and crystallize all reality into prismatic parts via symbol. If nothing more, poetry exists as the hoped for articulation of the reality we perceive and agree exists as well as the truest reality of being. Eventually the two are recognized as one – mind is recognized as the same substance we perceive.
Moreover, it is not beyond possibility that the most accurate articulation of this synthesis poetically objectifies what is commonly accepted as impossible; that is, absolute harmony of all seeming disparities. It is in this understanding via poetry

that the *logo*-as-word revivifies the miracle of faith; it moves to unify rather than question, extend rather than inhibit, expand rather than limit self- perception and substantiates a basic harmony between being and reality.

One could logically say the *logo* is that fragment cut loose from the tree of understanding, the inarticulate truth, the humanness that longs for contact with itself and the world. To know it is to be unimpeded on form, but fully in touch with meaning and content; to know what the Greeks knew as the One and Jesus identified as God. It is harmony of all things whether expressed as Pythagorean numerals, mathematically predictable music of the spheres, astrological charts of planetary alignments, the Hindu fire-rite at death, or the host raised high above the altar as the flesh of Jesus Christ, the most obvious incarnated *logo*-as-symbol. Yet behind the artificial and authoritarian formalization of spiritual illumination exists simply the word-as-*logo*, the vital symbol of all forces of being, all forces of the universe.

It is within reason to suggest that whatever lies within the realm of absolute faith is reality. By the same reasoning, poetry – the nearest articulation of mythic consciousness – becomes the vehicle by which every word becomes reality and vis versa. Yet all this talk of the *logo* presupposes some great psychic awakening; and from an exclusively linear point of view, it can be quite easily dismissed as mere words that have no real, innate reality to live out in the world; yet there is a pre-determinative factor in nature which can easily be assumed of everything related to our being.

Reason itself is the most obvious proof of the innate order of our design; yet the means to knowing that design is solely intuitional. It is logical to assume that any phenomena of being is totally reliant upon the rational and intuitional infrastructure of the human psyche; further, that any phenomena instigated or illuminated by language articulating unity of consciousness, if restricted in all its profoundly transformative aspects to the individual alone, cannot manifest as a collective awakening. In this respect, the institutionalization of spiritual life throughout history has been a gross distortion of each individual nature created, free and self-determinative.

Each individual contains all the *logoi* in the whole universe, but as Plotinus explains, the same *logoi* is not shared by all. Rather in respect to their individuality and their own self-realization, their differences are a result of different *logoi* or relativist truths in or out of sequence to the cosmos. Since the *logoi* resides in each individual as reflected by the nature of their mind, transformation is potentially forever in reach. "The whole revolution of the universe contains all the *logoi*," he writes, "and when it repeats itself it produces the same things again according to the same *logoi*. We ought not to be afraid of the infinity which this introduces into the intelligible world; for it is all in an indivisible unity and, we may say, comes forth when it acts."

If the *logo*, the word, does represent by nature the order of both being and reality, to what knowledge are we led? What realizations are — in our mechanistic concern for cause – being denied that, as a consequence, keeps us chained to strictly linear methods of understanding?

There are, I believe, only two things – harmony of being and harmony of purpose. Since the *logo* belongs to the intuitional matrix of the mind, it is the key to the individual phenomena. Without it we are nothing because as invoked by words, it makes logical all the various aspects of being, seeking harmony of all parts, revealing its infinite mystery and potential. It places us securely in the entire flow of natural process and affirms that we are – whether perceived or not – squarely in the inexorable movement of forces that – whether created by us or not – are mutually alike. Without absolute freedom, this fusion cannot occur, providing little hope of modern society finding affirmation of this harmony with all others.

The whole of Western civilization pretends to reflect unity of its parts, but its disunity has been apparent for so long that, with the homogenization of societies, the increasing restrictions of personal freedom, disunity is popularly and intellectually accepted as natural, all as a result of humanity's addiction to authoritarianism in every conceivable form and variation. It was no felicitous observation of Alcmaeon sometime at the beginning of the 5th century B.C. that "men perish because they cannot join the beginning to the end."

Perhaps it was Salvatore Dali who, by what he called his "paranoic-critical method" most powerfully shattered the decaying, spiritual sensibilities lying dormant and diseased in Western culture. By so doing, he showed very clearly the living result of spiritual atrophy reaching for definition in the 20th century. In painting after painting, in one schizophrenic, but highly realized deformation of metaphor, we come to realize the tragedy of humanity's 20th century loss, the twisted essence of nature, symbol and self in the modern age.

It matters not that sex or obsession dictates the universe. What is important to see is that within the context of his vision the *logo*-as imperfect-child is given caesarean birth, letting loose every conceivable pain without redemption, except as ejaculation. Dali's fantastic imagery is given such clarified reality that we accept it thoroughly as it horrifically deals with distortion of self as metaphor. What is evident is the challenge which he met and to which he sacrificed himself; that is, the very poetical dream of synthesis of *logo*, of symbol. No living artist has yet to equal the visual acuity he saw in this matter. And yet our living tragedy is that no poet no matter how professedly contemporary has broken the barrier to this integrative universe of being and by so doing found the world still intact. In describing what he called the "phenomenal architecture" of modern style, Dali described perfectly the rampant nature of the dilemma:

Deep depreciation of intellectual systems, highly accentuated depression of the reasoning activity to a degree bordering on mental debility, a positive lyrical imbecility, total aesthetic unconsciousness and no lyrical-religious coaction; on the other hand, there is release, freedom, development of unconscious mechanisms, ornamental automatism, stereotype, neologisms, great childhood neurosis, refuge in ideal worlds, hatred of reality, delusions of grandeur, perverse megalomania, need and feeling for the fanciful and hyper-aesthetic originality, shamelessness of pride, frenzied exhibitionism of caprice and imperialist fantasy, no notion of restraint, realization of solidified desires and majestic blooming with erotic, irrational, unconscious tendencies.

As coda to this description, he adds what he calls a "psycho-pathological parallel" which includes even more characteristics – dementia praecox, close affinities with the dream-world, reveries, waking fantasies, oneiric elements with such various manifestations as the anal-sadistic complex, what he called "flagrant ornamental coprophagia," and a "very slow, exhausting onanism," accompanied by an enormous sense of guilt.

Dali concluded that modern art had what he termed a "mania" for the "sterilized cleanliness" of functional forms and asceptic surfaces, admitting he could only paint according to certain systems of what he termed "digestive delirium.

Primalists might argue this is exactly the state to which all symbolization has taken us, reducing us to a state even further removed from innate purity of instinct and consciousness. This would be true if the very existence of language itself was completely unnatural as a human phenomena. But as can be shown in even cursory study of religious texts as well as poetry, articulated words spring, not from actual conscious need, rather from what is most unconscious to the human mind – its natural propensity out of which we are able to understand and express the phenomena of the living, human experience.

Folklore, anthropological studies, and treatises on shamanistic healing reveal that vital words and images as well as parts of magical rites as medical lore were generally kept secret, for by revealing destroyed their effectiveness on reality. For example, in a Kabbalistic vision of the Middle Ages, a great heap of Hebrew letters awaits the creation of the world, for not until all creation is performed will the letters describe everything falling into place, eventually forming the words of the Torah.

The ancient Egyptians believed words were virtually unlimited in power, and used to aid or influence nearly every major or minor event in their lives, though requiring expression in a formal voice. The Assyrians and Babylonians left a series of tablets that record various incantations thought necessary to keep human beings free of disease and the natural order together.

In relating the myth of Prometheus and Epimetheus in his dialogue *Protagoras*, Plato pointed out that man shared equal position with the gods because of divine kinship, but most importantly because of man's discovery of articulate speech, which at once allowed him to provide for themselves on earth, but showed their equality and kinship with the gods who favored their creation.

Alkindi, one of the great Arabic scholars of the early Middle Ages, claimed that through proper visualization of the imagination, it was possible to form thoughts capable of affecting any physical reality when accompanied by "solemnity, firm faith and strong desire," their effect heightened if these thoughts were spoken under favorable astrological conditions. According to Alkindi, the four basic elements were even affected by different voices, some influencing fire, others trees, or a particular tree; motion started, accelerated or impeded by words, animal life generated or destroyed, images made to appear in mirrors, flames and lightning produced, and other feats and illusions presumably all capable of being brought alive through the power of words.

If one momentarily discards the overt anthropomorphisms of Biblical rhetoric, one sees the Christian word synonymous with God, or creation. "In the beginning was the Word, and the Word was with God, and the Word was God." (John 1:1). Several Psalms indicate a relationship between creation and the utterance of the word. "For he spoke, and it came to be; he commanded and it stood forth." (Psalm xxxiii. 9). "He sent forth his word, and healed them, and delivered them from destruction." (Psalm cvii. 20).

It is interesting also to note two particular instances wherein Jesus himself makes significant reference to the Word both as stated and symbolic phenomena. In his parable of the power, Jesus states that for those who do not hear and understand the "word of the kingdom," or because of the word experience "tribulation or persecution," whatever man inherently possesses, whatever is "sown in his heart" will be taken away. (Matthew13:18-22) "He who hears the word and understands it; he indeed bears fruit, and yields." (Matthew13:23). The symbolic significance of the word is borne out even more strikingly by Jesus himself when, asked to judge a woman caught in adultery, twice bends to the ground and writes, though what he wrote is never recorded.

There are interesting associations inherent to these comments and acts, symbolic or otherwise. One certainly is the connection Jesus seems to make between knowledge of the word and entering the kingdom of heaven; that knowledge of the word is contingent to knowing the kingdom of heaven; perhaps not remaining knowledge, but finally the simple, self-reflection of what is the purest innocence within us. God may very well be only the metaphysical personification of all the creative and transformative properties of nature; in each of us it may be exemplified by our thought alone, capable of creation, order and harmony, characteristics indigenous to the word, forever fusing matter and process.

Is this the ultimate wisdom Jesus was talking about when brought children to touch? "Truly I say to you, whoever does not receive the kingdom of God like a child shall not enter it." (Matthew 10:15)

In what are called *The Forgotten Books of Eden* — books of the Old and New Testament written primarily during the Greek Hasmonean and Roman periods between 200 B.C. and 100 A.D., derived from later copies in their original languages of either Hebrew, Aramaic or Greek, and falsely ascribed to various biblical personalities, preserved by the early Catholic Church, but not accepted into standard biblical literature – one sees an interesting variation on the significance of the word-as-*logo*.

In *The Book of Adam and Eve*, a work of unknown Egyptian origin, but of which parts are found in the Talmud and Koran, it is related that when God saw Adam and Eve in their fallen state before the gate of the garden, rather than casting them out forever, he raised them from their fallen state by intoning his Word, "...the Word that created thee, and against which thou hast transgressed, the Word that made thee come out of the garden, and that raised thee when thou wast fallen."

The standard Book of Genesis describes God bringing every beast and bird for Adam to see and name at the beginning, sharing his power of creation through the Word, yet in his fallen state, rather than saving him, God condemns him with that very same power of word. "I will multiply your pain in childbearing," he said to Eve, and to Adam— "Cursed is the ground because of you; in toil you shall eat of it of the days of your life; thorns and thistles it shall bring forth to you... you are dust, and to dust you shall return."

In contrast, the Gnostic Gospels of the Nag Hammadi Library add an intriguing insight into this question of signification given the *logo*; it is seen as a deeper, more transcendent understanding, "cause of a system, which has been destined to come about." The "divine Logos" is synonymous with the nature of God, the Father, bringing forth the elements involved in creation, mankind being divided into three essential types – the spiritual, the psychic, and the material – conforming to what they considered the "triple arrangement of the Logos."

"Become earnest about the word," Jesus advises in the *Apocryphon of James*. "For...its first part is faith, the second love, the third works; for from these come life. For...when someone had sown it, he had faith in it; and when it sprouted, he loved it...So also can you yourselves receive the kingdom of heaven.."

In the case of Mohammed, the question of word-signification rests exclusively on the revelations and commands he received periodically from God via the angel Gabriel, every word of divine origin, eternal and "uncreate," or ever-existent as God himself. Although Mohammed is said to have neither been able to read nor write, it is interesting to note his revelations were themselves called in the Koran "Kitab," i.e. "what is written," or "scriptures." Gabriel himself is recorded as saying to Mohammed: "Recite! For thy Lord is beneficent. It is He who hath taught (to write) with the pen."

Brancusi rightly pointed out that the religious symbol – what I am identifying as the word-as-*logo* – reveals the solidarity existing between the structure of human existence and cosmic structures. Man is open to the world which becomes familiar to him through the symbol. It follows, he adds, that "he who understands a symbol not only gains access to an objective world," but simultaneously succeeds in withdrawing from his situation as an individual, entering into a state of "universal comprehension," the individual experience animated and transmuted into a "spiritual act."

Ernst Cassirer explains the phenomena of the word, much as a god or daemon, confronting man not as a something of his own creation, but existing in its own right as an objective reality. As soon as emotion finds its expression in the word or a mythic image, a turning point occurs. The purely subjective state vanishes, resolving itself in the objective myth or spoken word, allowing – as Cassirer points out –an "ever-progressive objectification" to begin.

This "ever-progressive objectification" reforms the cultural inheritance of the past into new, symbolic significance through each successive generation i.e. Roman integration of Greek sensibility, reexamination of classicism in the Renaissance combined with Christianity's cosmology of man and nature, the world view of 17th century Enlightenment aptly illustrated in the geometric gardens of Versailles. And Romanticism's re-dignifying of man, reabsorbing classicism to fit the demands of an ever advancing objectification of the human experience.

In each case, the word is recreated, metaphors are revised, the word makes its way unerringly back to that which is most expressively pure, most expressively accurate, the *logo*-as-articulated-science. It becomes the point of objectification, broadening our perception and understanding through finalized formation. Without the riveting harmony of the word, all experience would drop away in a discontinuous line of mere sense impressions. Here in its rawest form the progression from an at first inarticulate, self-illumination to articulated word knowledge, containing the germ of what I consider the profoundest literate understanding, that is, the word-as-*logo* binding two worlds, the purest, inexpressible, human experience with the synthetic dynamic of thought, and in that marriage capable of transforming the world.

If we could extend our vision as far down into the micro as possible, and as far above into the macro – as physically possible, or even useful, this may be – it is only poetry that can, perhaps through the prism of its imagery and conceptual synthesis, catch these infinite reflections of being and its possibilities, like mirrors catching the fullest eclipse of the sun. However, the metaphysical, spiritual, and philosophical import of the word has since undergone an incredible reduction in effect, so much so that even as representative of religious phenomena – assuming there is such as codified in the world's sacred books—no greater freedom has arisen from them, except endless stricture on the individual mind, changing nothing, representing nothing in the modern world except a collectivism of conscience, no more freeing the individual than actually preserving spiritual and social totalitarianism.

It is on this stage poetry plays out its soundless notes of self-doubt with absolutely no cognizance of its own meaning, purpose or potential; it is a reduced, human phenomena of the word that no longer connects to any innate knowledge or understanding of the self or the universe; it is, in short, a convenient outlet for a kind of neurologic *angst* buried in formalistic exercises of self-immolation.

This condition is even more evident in modern art that condones a general malaise of purposelessness. An art exhibition in 2012 at the Museum of Contemporary Art in Chicago, for example, described works on display as "like a body haunted by a phantom limb and the instinctive urge to use it," and that painters today are finding ways to "maintain a critical distance from the hand even as its presence is hard to deny." Another artist's work is described as allowing viewers to "foreground their relationship to the human body" and as a consequence "question their perceptions of how they inhabit their own bodies and identities."

"I feel the world is now in such bad shape that the interior liberty of the artist is a pretty trivial area," writes one contemporary artist. "Communal and social values are now more important. What office workers do in their lunch hour is more important than my pushing the limits of self-expression."

Obviously, words like these are soaked in the radiating effects of a rather poisonous, socialist ethic. In its so-called benevolent attempt to remarry form with content, it has made a cult out of divorcing the two, making it nearly impossible to know where outright distortion of real human realities end and truth begins. What is left is simply function without meaning, humanless invention, and creativity without ideational or spiritual synthesis.

As one of the more well-known, contemporary poets of the day admits – "With minimalist art we've finally reached the *reductio ad absurdum* of the whole modernist movement. Now we have cutting edge that's so finely honed there is nothing left for it to cut." It is fortunately easier to endure this cutting edge more in the visual arts than anywhere else, for the simple reason that as one fatigues of the meaningless and non-connectedness of its images and forms, one can simply turn away, but with language this cannot be done. The word demands its inheritance from the beginning, and if denied can, in the same respect, become a burden of mind-numbing symbols functioning without inherent order.

Certainly the madness of the 20th century was a direct result of the arbitrary and coercive limitation of freedom. As a consequence, we are left to speculate not on any outward symbol of integrative harmony of mind, body and culture, but only on the speculative inner world of Jungian archetypes and personal fantasy, all distorted, all no nearer a cultural reflection of knowledgeable integration on any but the most private level.

The lack of true freedom allows for nothing, but a socially conditioned conformity of response, not unity as a result of common agreement or propensity. In the modern age, the *logo* has been reduced to the ultimate in superficialities – political catch phrases, catchy advertising, trite choruses of popular songs spreading repetitive and pre-digested emotion, the latest best seller in popular psychology, obscurant poetry of strictly in-bred intellectualism preoccupied solely with form and the nightmares of personal anxieties.

In addition, we have conventional, religious beliefs that have lost any semblance of that "ever-progressive objectification" of the realities of being and world, insisting on their perpetuity, though having outlived their conceptual relevance by holding to their self-endowed authenticity. Suffering and alienation are the only symbols that are relevant to an age that, through its political barbarisms, accepts fragmentation as the price exacted by a so-called indifferent universe. The very spiritual apparatus responsible for building a new symbolic reference is castrated in all but the most stalwart and idealistic.

Nevertheless, underlying all this cheapening of language, the religious experience, the arts and modern life in general is the clear, simple, inter-connectedness of all things. With no superimposition of any kind, the realization of self which we seek to extend into the world meets nature on an equal footing, automatically destroying the naive concept of social planning, a concept that constantly positions humanity for any manipulation desired by the power structure of the time.

What is distilled from the profusion of modern conflicts, expedient ideologies, human unhappiness, and exploited human resources is the single poetic word of the defiant, poetic mind whose conscience and perception refuses to die. The systematic destruction of the Russian intelligentsia after 1917, and throughout the Twenties and Thirties, bears out in agonizing clarity this fear of the word, the *logo* assuming its rightful existence in the world.

Bitterly awakened to his inevitable fate, the Russian poet Osip Mandelstam – who wrote in 1921 that the word had entered a "heroic era" – wrote ten years later and a mere seven years before he was to die in one of Stalin's slave labor camps – "I have no manuscripts, no notebooks, no archives. I have no handwriting, for I never write. I alone in Russia work with my voice ... No matter how hard I work, whether I carry a horse slung across my shoulders, whether I turn millstones, no matter what I do, I shall never become a worker. My work, regardless of the form, is considered mischief, lawlessness, mere accident. But I like it that way, and I agree to my calling. I'll even sign my name with both hands."

Is the psychic, poetic drama that dangerous its mere presence in the world is a threat to stability? If the accumulated mass of scientific equations are now only worth saving, to whom can these possibly be important if the individual mind is destroyed? As long as the word is reduced to insignificance, history does not exist, and we also are made ostensibly nonexistent. Since the question is one of poetic fidelity, that is, faithfulness in the use of the word as reflective of truth, then one can easily claim the paramount importance of nothing less than completely revised expectations of poetry which must, more logically and rightly, be called religio-mystic by nature, all things real and abstract, presenting no risk to our perception of reality or our perception of being.

If we are to reach a new symbolic reference point, logically it must start in the liberated, poetic mind touched only by the unpolluted and uncorrupted source of real being where the cultivation of word and reality take on new significance. The repeated mistake that implies the individual no longer represents the true metaphoric measurement of humanity's substance is the key lie of modern rhetoric. Without the continuation of this lie, individual minds could not be shackled to stupidities, faithlessness, and cruelty. It is precisely this reduction to a socialist ethos that has seemingly done the most damage to the truly poetic mind. For in modern society, edict coldly moves the crushing stone into place, and the new, logical synthesis of metaphor is but the vague glimmer of nervous tension in the average, artistic mind solely interested in form.

What is the poet's fate in a world that plays duplicitous games of life and death over vast populations? To suggest the integrative capacity of a poet's thought can breach the walls of spiritual lies is realistic only to the extent they find new metaphoric meaning in their own life. It is what one could term the implicit goal of poetry to withstand the destruction of natural order; to play against the odds of insignificance; to bind the various disparities of the world on its physical as well as spiritual planes; to be the morphology by which the human mind recognizes the organic integrity of all things; and at the same time challenge the multitude of linguistic inaccuracies and institutional manipulations that have successfully reduced humanity to no more than over-civilized primitives, no less than spiritual masochists.

Because of our decreasing perimeter of human liberty, the world has proceeded to a peculiarly self-destructive, dualistic, psychic drama condition aptly described by Gabriel Marcel as "the refusal to reflect" and "the refusal to imagine." In this respect, one could say the Surrealist insistence on the absolute, liberating force of the imagination is the last option in order to retrieve what Andre Breton called the "primary freedom of experience."

"It (experience) paces back and forth in a cage from which it is more and more difficult to make it emerge. It too leans for support on what is most immediately expedient, and it is protected by the sentinels of common sense. Under the pretense of civilization and progress, we have managed to banish from the mind everything that may rightly or wrongly be termed superstitious, or fancy; forbidden is any kind of search for truth which is not in conformance."

A clear danger to any significant cultural evolution of the imagination is insidiously demonstrated in what some psychologists now call "nature deficit disorder." So disconnected are those in continual application of digital frames of reference that one consumer psychologist explained that these 21st century habitués of the digital world now find the artificial "ever so slightly more real" and that "things that are tangible . . . may have lost some of their allure."

Whatever becomes of Western civilization, there is no question its fate is intimately tied to the fate of the word as carrier of what we come to understand in the future; it offers no less than liberty, no more than the purest idealism of intent. At both extremes they balance precariously alive, precariously beautiful in the hypocrisy of the modern age.

The Nobel Prize-winning poet, Salvatore Quasimodo, expressed the possible future rather sadly, fully cognizant of the potential outcome of our situation. "If the tedium of listening to man's heart is now at its limit of endurance... if the 'object' of the artisan created by many hands is of greater value than one created by the spirit of a few lost men, who are after all those who create culture, then with the poets banished from the earth like a 'great plague,' the time of silence will arrive."

We have been pushed to the extreme end and beginning of a new poetic which will eventually correspond to a new age of faith. With the demise of faithlessness will emerge, as a consequence, a poetic of clean reduction to meaning, fused again to the word which, once becoming dynamic, has no equal to faith; it is in effect the renaming of the world, weighing heavily each fragment made to bear the last Sisphyean mile, until it finds itself re-empowered with the basic psychology of our humanness. This reductionism will not be so much in form as in the rediscovered dynamics of thought related to what the word initially represented at an earlier, more spiritually cognizant age wherein thought and action were more readily fused as one and the same. One appreciation of this new union will be most readily discerned in a more harmonious synthesis of forms both intellectual and perceptual.

In our cauldron of aliteracy, perhaps shuffled away in some corner of the world is a manuscript more illuminating than anything with which we are familiar, a poet more courageous and intelligent than we imagine exists in modern society. Civilization as we understand it rests in that poet's hands; yet without their dialogue of modern conscience, we do not hear the dying and the survival, without the character of the poet's love no transformative word.

If it has to matter the word will find its way back to meaning, its clairvoyance of purpose through the poet's voice. Though they may be crying, tears will not come, except as living rivers of pain. Though the sound of computers buries ever deeper the human identity, the word will find its way back to meaning again to smile the giving, to form the idea of being again.

References

The Imperative

Eugen Herrigal. *The Method of Zen.* New York: Vintage Books, 1960. 71.

Jose Ortega y Gasset. *The Dehumanization of Art and Other Essays on Art, Culture, and Literature*. Princeton, NJ: Princeton University Press:1968.18+10.

Ernest Cassirer. *Language and Myth.* Translated by Susanne K. Langer New York: Dover Publications, 1946.7+36.

Heraclitus. *Ancilla and the Pre-Socratic Philosophers.* Translated by Kathleen Freeman. Cambridge: Harvard University Press, 1948. 24–34.

Why We Alone Live

Heraclitus. *Ancilla and the PreSocratic Philosophers.* Translated by Kathleen Freeman. Cambridge: Harvard University Press, 1948. 24-34.

Osip Mandelstam. "The Word and Culture,"*Complete Critical Prose* Ed. Jane Gary Harris. Translated by Jane Gary Harris and Constance Link. Dana Point, California: Ardis. 1997. 71.

Alexander Konstantinovich Gladkov. *Meetings With Pasternak: A Memoir*. New York: Harcourt, Brace, Jovanovich, 1977.

On the Difficulties of Poetry in Translation

Peter France. "Baudelaire," *The Oxford Guide to Literature in English Translation.* Oxford: Oxford University Press, 2000. 285.

Susan Sontag. *Where the Stress Falls: Essays.* NewYork: Farrar, Straus, and Giroux, 2001.

Illan Stavans. *Eight Conversations.* Madison: University of Wisconsin Press, 2004.

Eliot Weinberger. *Introduction to Altazoror A Voyage in a Parachute*, A poem in VII Cantos by Vincente Huidobro. Saint Paul, Minnesota: Graywolf Press, 1988. viii.

The Fate of the Word

Heraclitus. *Ancilla and the Pre-Socratic Philosophers.* Translated by Kathleen Freeman. Cambridge: Harvard University Press, 1948. 24–34.

Plotinus. *Plotinus.* New York: Collier Books, Crowell-Collier Publishing Co. 1962.77.

Alcmaeon. *Ancilla and the Pre-Socratic Philosophers.* Translated by Kathleen Freeman. Cambridge: Harvard University Press, 1948. 40.

Salvatore Dali. *Dali on Modern Art: The Cuckolds of Antiquated Modern Art.* Translated by Haaken M. Cevalier. New York: The Dial Press, 1957. 41+43/ also later quotes 51+81.

Lynnn Thorndike. "Egyptians" and "Alkindi" in *A History of Magic and Experimental Science During the First Thirteen Centuries of Our Era*. Vol. 1. New York: Columbia Univ. Press 1923.10 +644-45.

Plato. *Protagoras*. Translated by Robert C. Bartlett. Harmondsworth, Middlesex, England: Penguin, 2006.

Rutherford Hayes Platt, J. Alden Brett and Paul Laure. *The Forgotten Books of Eden*. New York: Bell Publishing Co. 1980.

"The Tripartite Tractate," *The Nag Hammadi Library*. Ed. James M. Robinson. New York: Harper & Row, 1981. 68.

"Apocryphon of James," *The Nag Hammadi Library*. 32-33

The Koran. Translated by N.J. Dawood. Harmondsworth, Middlesex, England: Penguin, 1956. 208.

Sir William Muil.*The Life of Mohammed*. Edinburgh: John Grant, 1923.

Lonel Jianou. *Brancusi*. New York: Tudor Publishing Co. 1963. 151.

Ernest Cassirer. *An Essay on Man: An Introduction to a Philosophy of Human Culture*. Garden City, New York: Anchor Doubleday & Co. 1944. 82.

Michael Darling. "Phantom Limb: Approaches to Painting Today" and Naomi Beck "Jimmy Robert Vis-à-vis."MCA Chicago, Exhibition catalog, Summer, 2012. 11 + 21.

Douglas C. McGill. "Sculpture Goes Public." *New York Times Magazine*, April 27, 1986. quoting Scott Burton. 67.

Ron Grossman. "Ferlinghetti's U.S. Canvas: A Portrait of Poetic Passion." *Chicago Tribune*, May 19,1986, quoting Lawrence Ferlinghetti. Sec. 5, 3.

Gabriel Marcel. *Mystery of Being*, vol. 1. "Reflection & Mystery." Chicago, Illinois: Gateway Edition, Henry Regnery Co. 1960. 44.

Andre Breton. *Manifestoes of Surrealism*. Translated by Richard Seaves and Helen R. Lane. Ann Arbor, Michigan: University of Michigan Press, 1969. 10.

Bruce Horovitz. "Artificial Christmas Tree Sales are Growing." *USA Today*, Nov. 30, 2012, quoting Kit Yarrow, consumer psychologist, 3A.

Salvatore Quasimodo. *The Selected Writings of Salvatore Quasimodo*. Edited and translated by Allen Mandelbaum. New York: Minerva Press, 1960.

www.ingramcontent.com/pod-product-compliance
Lightning Source LLC
Chambersburg PA
CBHW030532310726
48979CB00010B/1888/J

* 9 7 8 0 9 6 2 5 3 0 6 9 2 *